T0390182

 **SPACE-LICIOUS!** ⭐ **Out-of-This-World Recipes** 🚀

CREATE!

SPACE TRAVEL

SPACE-THEMED RECIPES

by Jane Yates

BEARPORT
PUBLISHING

Minneapolis, Minnesota

Credits
Cover and title page, © olgaarkhipenko/Adobe Stock and © Yeti Studio/Adobe Stock and © Anoly_D/Adobe Stock and © 3000ad/Adobe Stock and © Tanya_mtv/Shutterstock; Background images, flashmovie/Adobe Stock; Lifestyle Graphic/Adobe Stock; 6 bottom left, NASA/Public Domain; 6 bottom right, 3000ad/Adobe Stock; 8 left, NASA/Crew of STS-132/Public Domain; 10 bottom, NASA/Public Domain; 14 bottom left, NASA Johnson Space Center/Public Domain; 16 bottom left, Bjoertvedt/Creative Commons; 18 bottom right, NASA/David Scott/Public Domain; p 22 top right, Edgar D. Mitchell /NASA/Public Domain; all other photos ©Austen Photography

Bearport Publishing Company Product Development Team
Publisher: Jen Jenson; Director of Product Development: Spencer Brinker; Editorial Director: Allison Juda; Editor: Cole Nelson; Editor: Tiana Tran; Production Editor: Naomi Reich; Art Director: Kim Jones; Designer: Kayla Eggert; Designer: Steve Scheluchin; Production Specialist: Owen Hamlin

Statement on Usage of Generative Artificial Intelligence
Bearport Publishing remains committed to publishing high-quality nonfiction books. Therefore, we restrict the use of generative AI to ensure accuracy of all text and visual components pertaining to a book's subject. See BearportPublishing.com for details.

Produced for Bearport Publishing by BlueAppleWorks Inc.
Managing Editor for BlueAppleWorks: Melissa McClellan
Art Director: T.J. Choleva
Photo Research: Jane Reid

Library of Congress Cataloging-in-Publication Data is available at www.loc.gov or upon request from the publisher.

ISBN: 979-8-89577-034-4 (hardcover)
ISBN: 979-8-89577-151-8 (ebook)

For more information, write to Bearport Publishing, 3500 American Blvd W, Suite 150, Bloomington, MN 55431.

CONTENTS

SPACE-LICIOUS!

Let's learn about space and cooking at the same time! How would you like to try a moon cake or sip your very own homemade rocket fuel? With this book, you can make six delicious, out-of-this-world recipes. Let's blast off!

Measuring liquid ingredients

- Use a measuring cup with a spout. This makes it easier to pour liquids without spilling.

- Always set the measuring cup on a flat surface.

- When adding liquid, bend down so your eye is level with the measurement markers on the cup to be sure you have the right amount.

Measuring dry ingredients

- Scoop the ingredients with the correct size measuring cup or measuring spoon.

- Level off the top with the back of a butter knife or another straight edge to make sure you get the right amount every time.

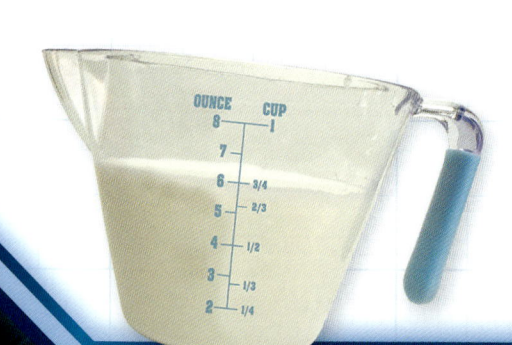

Ingredients

Most of these recipes can be made with things you probably already have in your kitchen. Before you start each recipe, make sure you have all the ingredients you need. It's a good idea to set your ingredients and tools on the counter before you begin.

Microwave safety

Each microwave works a little differently, so ask an adult to help show you how to use yours. Be sure to use only dishes that are safe for the microwave, such as glass or ceramic. Never use metal or aluminum foil in the microwave. After cooking, carefully check that a dish isn't too hot before taking it out.

Allergy Alert!

Recipes that include the common allergens wheat, eggs, and dairy are marked with a special symbol. Please use a safe **substitute** ingredient if you need to.

 Wheat   Eggs

 Dairy

 **BE SAFE!** Always ask for an adult's help with knives and when using the oven or stove.

FRUITY ROCKETSHIP

Since we first started sending people into space, we have used rockets. Hot gases pushing out the bottom of the rockets give them the power to escape Earth's **gravity**. Their long, smooth, **cylindrical** shape helps the vehicles smoothly cut their way through the air. Make a fruity rocket snack to give you energy to blast off into your day!

Ingredients

* Cantaloupe or other melon
* 2 strawberries
* 1 banana

Equipment

* A cutting board
* A butter knife
* A 4-in. (10-cm) wooden stir stick or skewer

Apollo 11 was the first mission to land humans on the moon. Its rocket launched on July 16, 1969.

Scientists are working on new tech to send people farther into space.

1 Ask an adult to help you cut a piece of cantaloupe into a block that is about 2 in. (5 cm) long, 1 in. (2.5 cm) wide, and ½ in. (1.3 cm) thick. Then, cut a jagged edge into one side of the cantaloupe to make a flame shape.

2 Next, wash and dry your strawberries. Carefully cut the leaves off the top of the berries. Slice one of the strawberries into disks about ¼ in. (0.6 cm) wide.

3 Peel the banana and cut a handful of slices, each about ¼ in. (0.6 cm) thick.

4 Next, push the mostly whole strawberry onto the end of a stir stick, stopping before you reach the tip. Slide a slice of banana onto the stick up to the strawberry, followed by a slice of strawberry.

5 Keep adding banana and strawberry slices, **alternating** them.

6 Finally, push the cantaloupe piece onto the stick to finish your rocket. If you need more of a boost, use the rest of the banana and more strawberries to make another fruit rocket snack!

SPACE BERRIES

When the United States space agency known as NASA gets food ready for space, it can be complicated. They need to prepare the food so it takes up very little space, lasts a long time, and still keeps its **nutrients**. Sometimes, astronaut food is **dehydrated** using heat. Try making your own dehydrated strawberries ready to eat in space!

Ingredients

* About 12 strawberries

Equipment

* A baking sheet
* Parchment paper
* A butter knife
* A fork

Astronauts on the International Space Station (ISS) sometimes get fresh food, but they usually eat dehydrated meals and snacks.

1. **Preheat** the oven to 200°F (90°C), and line a baking sheet with parchment paper.

2. Wash and dry the strawberries. Then, use a butter knife to carefully slice them into pieces about ¼ in. (0.6 cm) thick. Discard the tops and the ends.

3. Next, lay the strawberry slices on the prepared baking sheet.

4. With an adult's help, put the baking sheet in the oven and bake the strawberries for 2 hours.

5. Ask an adult to remove the baking sheet from the oven. Use a fork to carefully peel the strawberry slices off the paper and flip them over.

6. Ask an adult to put the baking sheet back in the oven and bake for another 30 minutes, or until the strawberries are fully dried.

7. Ask an adult to remove the baking sheet from the oven and let the strawberries cool completely.

9

ASTRONAUT LUNCH

After NASA prepares food for astronauts, they package it. The wrappers are sometimes designed so astronauts can eat right out of them. This keeps food from floating away in the low gravity of space. Make your own foil-wrapped meal to eat lunch just like an astronaut.

Ingredients

* ¼ cup ketchup
* 1 Tbsp molasses
* 1 Tbsp maple syrup or honey
* 1 tsp lemon juice or vinegar
* A pinch of salt
* A pinch of black pepper
* Hot sauce (optional)
* A cooked chicken breast

Equipment

* A sheet of aluminum foil, about 11 x 12 in. (28 x 30 cm)
* A microwave-safe bowl
* A spoon
* A knife
* A fork

Astronauts on the ISS eat many meat and fish meals out of foil packages.

1 Start by making the space food pouch. Fold the piece of aluminum foil in half so the shorter sides meet.

2 With the open edge facing away from you, fold both of the layers on one of the sides by about ½ in. (1.3 cm) inward, toward the center. Repeat on other side. Then, fold each side inward two more times. Your pouch should now be about 7 in. (18 cm) wide.

3 To make the bottom of the pouch stronger, fold it up about ½ in. (1.3 cm) two times.

4 Finally, pull the open top of the pouch apart slightly to make it easier to place the food inside. Set the pouch aside.

5 Place the ketchup, molasses, maple syrup or honey, and the lemon juice or vinegar into a microwave-safe bowl. Add the salt and pepper.

6 Use a spoon to mix everything together until well blended. If you like things spicy, add a drop or two of hot sauce and taste until it's the right level of spice.

7 Ask an adult to use the knife to carefully cut the chicken.

8 Use a fork to pull apart the chicken into bite-sized pieces.

9 Place the chicken into the bowl with the sauce. Stir well with a spoon and let the mixture sit for a few minutes.

10 With an adult's help, microwave the bowl for 60 seconds. Ask an adult to carefully remove the bowl from the microwave, and let it cool slightly.

11 Use a spoon or fork to transfer the marinated chicken into the aluminum pouch. Enjoy your space meal like an astronaut on the ISS!

ROCKET FUEL

Just as rockets need fuel to blast off, human bodies need fuel to live and work. Why not fuel up with a delicious smoothie to give your body energy all day? If you were an astronaut, you would sip this drink from a pouch with a specially designed straw that keeps liquids from floating away.

Ingredients

- ½ cup strawberries, blueberries, or spinach
- 1 banana
- ½ cup milk
- ¼ cup plain yogurt

Allergy Alert!

Equipment

- A butter knife
- A blender
- A drinking glass
- A reusable straw (optional)

Some drinks are sent to space as a dry powder. Water is added later.

1 Decide if you want to make a strawberry, blueberry, or spinach smoothie. Measure about ½ cup of your choice. Then, use a butter knife to cut the banana into small pieces.

2 Pour the milk into the blender.

3 Next, add the yogurt to the blender, followed by the banana slices and the fruit or spinach.

4 Put the lid on the blender and blend for about 30 seconds, or until the ingredients are all mixed and the drink is smooth.

5 Pour your smoothie into a glass and enjoy! If you feel like drinking like an astronaut, add a straw!

ASTRONAUT ICE CREAM

When NASA tried to prepare ice cream for space, they froze it to −40°F (−40°C). Then, they heated it quickly to remove the water. Unfortunately, after all this, they found out the treat was too crumbly for space! Luckily, there's no reason you can't enjoy it on Earth.

Ingredients

* The whites from 2 large eggs
* ½ tsp lemon juice
* ⅛ tsp salt
* ½ cup sugar
* Food coloring
* Sprinkles

Allergy Alert!

Equipment

* A baking sheet
* Parchment paper
* A large mixing bowl
* A whisk
* A spoon

Astronaut ice cream became a popular souvenir treat in the 1970s.

1 Preheat the oven to 250°F (120°C) and line a baking sheet with parchment paper.

2 Add the egg whites, lemon juice, and salt into a large mixing bowl. **Whisk** the ingredients until they become **frothy**.

3 Gradually add the sugar, one spoonful at a time, while continuing to whisk.

4 Add two drops of food coloring and keep whisking until the mixture forms stiff peaks that stick to your whisk when lifted.

5 Drop large spoonfuls of the mixture onto the prepared baking sheet until it is all used. Decorate with sprinkles.

6 With an adult's help, place the baking sheet in the oven and bake for 35 minutes. Then, turn the oven off and leave the baking sheet in the oven for another hour.

7 Ask an adult to carefully remove the baking sheet from the oven. Let your astronaut ice cream cool completely, and enjoy your space treat!

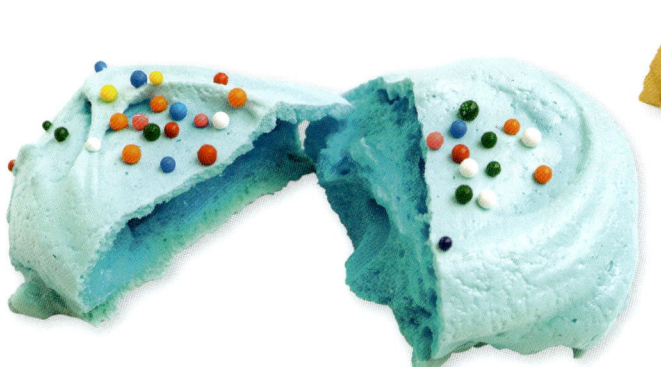

MOON CAKE

Between 1968 and 1972, six NASA missions landed humans on the moon. The 12 astronauts who were dropped there explored a lunar surface full of craters, valleys, and planes. Make your own moon cake and decorate its surface to look just like the moon!

Ingredients

For the Cake:
* 2 large eggs
* ½ cup sugar
* 1 tsp vanilla extract
* ¼ tsp salt
* 1 cup all-purpose flour
* 1 tsp baking powder
* ½ cup milk
* 1 Tbsp butter
* Several small chocolate cookies
* Assorted candies

For the Icing:
* ½ cup butter or margarine, softened
* 1 cup powdered sugar
* 1 Tbsp milk
* 1 tsp vanilla extract
* Food coloring

Allergy Alert!

Equipment

* 2 mixing bowls
* A whisk
* 2 microwave-safe bowls
* Spoons
* Parchment paper
* A toothpick
* A plate
* 1 small flag for decoration

Some astronauts drove lunar rovers on the moon.

Cake

1 In a mixing bowl, combine the eggs, sugar, vanilla, and salt. Whisk **vigorously** for about a minute.

2 Add the flour and baking powder to the bowl. Whisk until everything is well mixed.

3 In a small, microwave-safe bowl, combine the milk and butter. Microwave for 30 seconds, then remove and stir with a spoon. Repeat heating for 10 seconds at a time, stirring in between, until the butter is fully melted and blended with the milk.

4 Pour the milk and butter mixture into the bowl with the other ingredients. Whisk until the batter is smooth.

5 Line another microwave-safe bowl with parchment paper, leaving extra around the top. Then, pour the batter into it.

6 Microwave the batter for 1 minute and 30 seconds. Then, carefully check the cake by inserting a toothpick into the center. If the toothpick has wet batter on it, microwave for another 10 seconds at a time until the toothpick comes out clean. Ask an adult to remove the hot bowl from the microwave. Let the cake cool completely.

Icing

1 Use a spoon to beat the softened butter for about a minute. If you prefer, you can ask for an adult to help you use a hand mixer instead.

2 Add 1 cup of powdered sugar, a little at a time, stirring well after each addition.

3 Add the milk and vanilla extract. Stir until well mixed.

4 Add a few drops of food coloring and stir. Continue adding food coloring and stirring until you like the color.

5 Once the cake has fully cooled, carefully lift it out of the bowl using the parchment paper.

6 Place the cake upside down on a plate, and carefully peel off the parchment paper.

7 Use the back of a spoon to spread the icing evenly over the top.

8 Decorate the cake by pressing small chocolate cookies and candies into the icing to resemble craters. Break a few cookies into pieces and press them into the icing to look like moon rocks. Sprinkle any crumbs over the top.

9 Finally, place a small flag on top of the cake and enjoy!

MEET A HUNGRY ASTRONAUT

In 1961, Alan Shepard became the first American in space. He later served as commander of the Apollo 14 mission in 1971. On Earth, Shepard enjoyed watching the Houston Astros baseball team—named in honor of the city's NASA Johnson Space Center. While watching, he would grab a hot dog to eat.

Shepard standing beside a flag during the Apollo 14 mission

Make Space-licious Hot Dog Rockets

1 With an adult's help, open a biscuit or croissant dough package.

2 Use a butter knife to cut the dough into strips about ½ in. (1.3 cm) wide.

3 Push a skewer through each hot dog, leaving about 1 in. (2.5 cm) sticking out at both ends. Wrap the dough strips around the hot dogs.

4 Place the wrapped hot dogs on a baking sheet and bake for 12 minutes at 400°F (200°C). Let the hot dogs cool, then add cheese triangles to both ends and enjoy!

GLOSSARY

alternating taking turns, first one then the other

cylindrical having a three-dimensional shape with a curved surface and round top and bottom, like a tube or a can

dehydrated dried out or having all the water removed

frothy having lots of tiny bubbles of air from stirring

gravity a force that pulls objects toward the ground or attracts them toward one another

nutrients vitamins, minerals, and other substances needed by living things for health and growth

preheat to heat in advance to a set temperature

souvenir something you buy or keep to remember a special trip, place, or event

substitute a similar item used in place of another item

vigorously with lots of force and energy

whisk to mix liquid cooking ingredients using a quick, light whipping motion

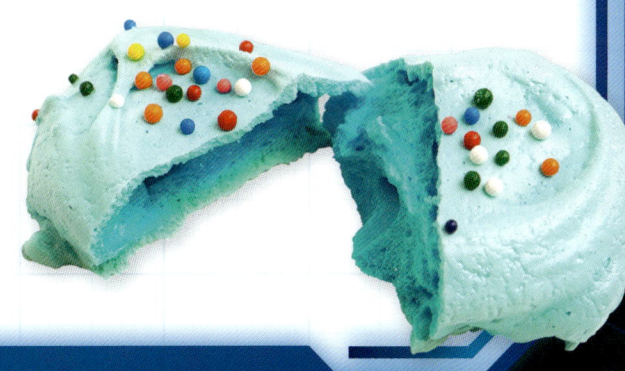

INDEX

READ MORE

Bailey, Diane. *Destination Moon (The Moon Files).* Minneapolis: Lerner Publications, 2025.

Kelley, K. C. *Space Careers (Jobs on the Edge).* Minneapolis: Bearport Publishing, 2025.

LEARN MORE ONLINE

1. Go to **FactSurfer.com** or scan the QR code below.

2. Enter **"Space Travel Recipes"** into the search box.

3. Click on the cover of this book to see a list of websites.

ABOUT THE AUTHOR

Jane Yates is an avid cook who worked in restaurants while attending art school. She has written more than 20 craft books for children.